PERSONAL STORIES

A Book For Adults
Who Are Beginning to Read

KAMLA DEVI KOCH

LINDA MROWICKI

ARLENE RUTTENBERG

Photography by:
Daniel C. Jackson

Illustrations by:
Sally Richardson

LINMORE PUBLISHING, INC.   P.O. BOX 1545   PALATINE, IL 60078

Linmore Publishing, Inc.
P.O. Box 1545
Palatine, IL 60078

© Linmore Publishing, Inc. 1985
   First printing, 1985   Printed in the United States of America
   Second printing, 1986

All rights reserved. No part of this book may be reproduced or transmitted in any form or by any means, electronic or mechanical, including photocopying, recording, or by any information storage or retrieval system without written permission from the publisher.

PERSONAL STORIES

Student's Book   ISBN 0-916591-0**2**-6
Teacher's Book   ISBN 0-916591-0**3**-4

ACKNOWLEDGEMENTS

The following people provided valuable assistance. We thank them for their patience, good humor, interest and enthusiasm in the project: **Erv and Theresa Barker; Andy, Nancy, Julie, and Tommy Cirmo; Jasmine Jessica Hunter; Anne, Robert, Jeanne, Mary, Scott, Harley, and Tom Jackson; John F. Knaff; Mrs. Robert Mosbach; Greg Morris; Genevieve, James, and Joseph Mrowicki; Bruce, Cathy, and Corinne Oswald; Anne Pica,** and **Mr. and Mrs. James Yaklich.**

We would also like to thank two people who participated in the field-testing; **Hermione Livermore**, Minneapolis Public Schools Adult and Continuing Education Program and **Clare F. O'Leary**, Refugee Education and Employment Program, Arlington, Virginia. They provided many excellent suggestions. Special thanks goes to all the students who used the materials and provided such positive feedback.

K.D.K.
L.M.
A.R.

We are grateful to **Mr. and Mrs. Sarwan Bhatty** for their support and encouragement.

K.D.K.
A.R.

I would like to thank my husband, **Dan Koch,** for his interest, enthusiasm, and wholehearted support.

K.D.K.

Except for the Grace and Fred McDonald lessons, all the characters are fictitious and any resemblance between the characters and the people in the photos is therefore coincidental.

TABLE OF CONTENTS

FAMILY

Joe Johnson 2

Maria Rosario 6

Grace McDonald 10

Bill Miller 14

Rose Sullivan 18

Tom Baker and Lisa Washington 22

HOME

Maria's House 28

Grace and Fred's House 32

Joe's Apartment 36

Rose's Mobile Home 40

Tom and Lisa's Condo 44

The Millers' Farm House 48

WEEKDAY ACTIVITIES

Joe's Day 54

Beth Miller's Day 58

Maria's Day 62

Grace's Day 66

Rose's Day 70

Lisa and Tom's Day 74

FAMILY

Important words:

family	grandparents	single
husband	grandmother	married
wife	grandfather	divorced
parents	grandchildren	
mother	grandson	
father	granddaughter	
children		
son		
daughter		
brother		
sister		

JOE JOHNSON

Hi.
I am Joe Johnson.
I am single.
I am 21 years old.

I come from a farm.
My family lives on the farm.
I live in the city.
I moved to the city 5 years ago.
The farm is far from the city.

I work in the city.
I like the city.
I like the people in the city.

CHECK YOUR UNDERSTANDING.

Read. Circle Yes or No.

1. This is Joe Jackson.   Yes   No
2. Joe is single.   Yes   No
3. Joe is married.   Yes   No
4. Joe is 20.   Yes   No

5. Joe lives on a farm.   Yes   No
6. Joe comes from a farm.   Yes   No
7. Joe's family lives on a farm.   Yes   No
8. Joe lives in the city.   Yes   No
9. Joe moved to the city.   Yes   No
10. The city is far from the farm.   Yes   No

11. Joe likes the city.   Yes   No
12. Joe works in the city.   Yes   No
13. Joe lives in the city.   Yes   No
14. Joe likes the people in the city.   Yes   No

WORD STUDY.

Read the story.

Write the words with F.

f _ _ _

f _ _ _

f _ _ _ _ _

f _ _

Write the missing letters. Copy the words.

far   f _ _   _____

farm   f _ _ m   _____

from   f _ _ m   _____

Write the correct words. Copy the sentences.

1. Joe comes _____ a farm.

   _____

2. Joe's family lives on the _____ .

   _____

3. The farm is _____ from the city.

   _____

4

AND YOU?

Read. Circle Yes or No.

1. I am single.   Yes   No
2. I am married.   Yes   No
3. I live in a city.   Yes   No
4. My family lives in a city.   Yes   No
5. I live on a farm.   Yes   No
6. My family lives on a farm.   Yes   No
7. I work in a city.   Yes   No
8. I work on a farm.   Yes   No

PERSONAL STORY.

Copy your Yes sentences.

_____

_____

_____

_____

_____

_____

_____

_____

MARIA ROSARIO

Hello.

My name is Maria Rosario.

I am 35 years old.

I am a teacher.

I am single.

Maybe I will have a husband someday.

I live in a house.

My parents live far away.

I have one brother.

His name is Robert.

He lives near our parents.

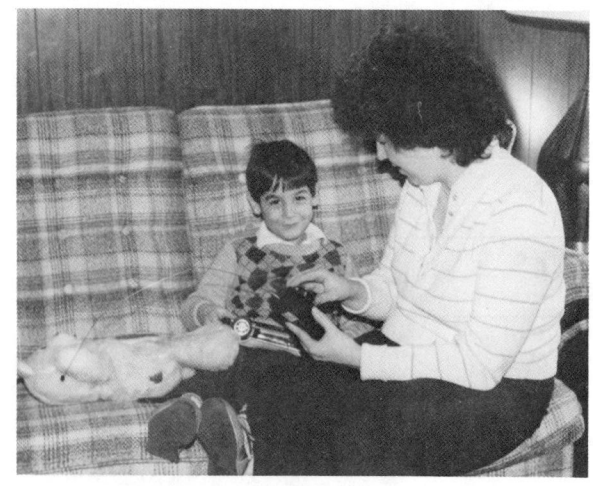

Robert is married.

He has a son.

His name is Tony.

I visit them on the weekend.

CHECK YOUR UNDERSTANDING.

Read. Circle Yes or No.

1. Maria is 36 years old.   Yes   No
2. Maria is a teacher.   Yes   No
3. Maria is married.   Yes   No
4. Maria is single.   Yes   No
5. Maria has a husband.   Yes   No

6. Maria lives in a house.   Yes   No
7. Maria has an apartment.   Yes   No
8. Maria has a brother.   Yes   No
9. Maria lives with her parents.   Yes   No
10. Maria lives near her parents.   Yes   No

11. Maria's brother is single.   Yes   No
12. Maria has a son.   Yes   No
13. Her brother's name is Tony.   Yes   No
14. Maria visits her brother on the weekend.   Yes   No

WORD STUDY.

Write the opposites.

daughter __ __ __

married __ __ __ __ __ __

far __ __ __ __

Write the correct words. Copy the sentences.

1. Her _____ is Maria.
          name   am

    _____

2. Maria is _____ years old.
          35   53

    _____

3. Maria is a _____ .
          teach   teacher

    _____

4. Maria lives _____ a house.
          in   on

    _____

5. Maria has _____ brother.
          one   on

    _____

6. _____ name is Robert.
      Is   His

    _____

AND YOU?

Read. Circle Yes or No.

1.	I am married.	Yes	No
2.	I am single.	Yes	No
3.	I have a husband.	Yes	No
4.	I have a wife.	Yes	No
5.	I live in a house.	Yes	No
6.	I live in an apartment.	Yes	No
7.	I live with my parents.	Yes	No
8.	I live near my parents.	Yes	No
9.	I live far from my parents.	Yes	No

PERSONAL STORY.

Copy your Yes sentences.

_____

_____

_____

_____

_____

_____

_____

_____

_____

GRACE McDONALD

I am Grace McDonald.
I am married.
I am 67 years old.
My husband is 65 years old.

My husband's name is Fred.
He does not work now.
He is retired.
He stays home.
He helps me.

We have a son and a daughter.
They do not live with us.
My daughter is 33 years old.
She lives in a house.
My son is 27 years old.
He lives in an apartment.
We do not have any grandchildren.

CHECK YOUR UNDERSTANDING.

Read. Circle Yes or No.

1. Grace is married.   Yes   No
2. Grace is 65 years old.   Yes   No
3. Grace's husband is 65 years old.   Yes   No

4. Fred is Grace's husband.   Yes   No
5. Fred works.   Yes   No
6. Fred is retired.   Yes   No
7. Fred helps Grace.   Yes   No

8. Fred and Grace have two children.   Yes   No
9. They have two daughters.   Yes   No
10. Their daughter is 33.   Yes   No
11. Their son is 27.   Yes   No
12. Their son lives in a house.   Yes   No
13. Their daughter lives in a house.   Yes   No
14. Grace and Fred have two grandchildren.   Yes   No

WORD STUDY.

Read the story.

Write the words with M.

```
M _ _ _ _ _ _
m _ _ _ _ _
m _
m _
```

Write the words with H.

```
h _ _ _ _ _
h _
h _ _
h _ _ _
h _ _ _
```

Write the sentences with different words.

1. <u>He</u> does not work now.

   _____

2. <u>He</u> stays home.

   _____

3. <u>He</u> helps <u>me.</u>

   _____

4. <u>They</u> do not live with <u>us.</u>

   _____

Write the sentences.

1. fred is grace's husband

   _____

2. he does not work now

   _____

12

AND YOU?

Read. Circle Yes or No.

1.	I am married.	Yes	No
2.	I am single.	Yes	No
3.	I am retired.	Yes	No
4.	I work.	Yes	No
5.	I stay home.	Yes	No
6.	I have a child.	Yes	No
7.	I have 2 children.	Yes	No
8.	I have 3 children.	Yes	No
9.	I have 4 children.	Yes	No
10.	I have many children.	Yes	No
11.	I have grandchildren.	Yes	No

PERSONAL STORY.

Copy your Yes sentences.

_____
_____
_____
_____
_____
_____
_____
_____

BILL MILLER

I am Bill Miller.

My wife's name is Faye.

We have two children.

Allen is 23 years old.

Beth is 18.

I am a farmer.

My grandfather gave the farm to my father.

My father gave the farm to me.

Allen likes the farm.

I will give the farm to him.

This is our daughter Beth.

Beth is pretty and smart.

She is engaged.

CHECK YOUR UNDERSTANDING.

Read. Circle Yes or No.

1.	Bill is married.	Yes	No
2.	Mrs. Miller's name is Faye.	Yes	No
3.	Bill and Faye have children.	Yes	No
4.	Bill is 32 years old.	Yes	No
5.	Beth is 18 years old.	Yes	No
6.	Bill is a farmer.	Yes	No
7.	Bill's father was a farmer.	Yes	No
8.	Bill's grandfather was a farmer.	Yes	No
9.	Bill will give the farm to his son.	Yes	No
10.	Allen likes the farm.	Yes	No
11.	Bill and Faye have a daughter.	Yes	No
12.	Their son's name is Beth.	Yes	No
13.	Beth is pretty.	Yes	No
14.	Beth is smart.	Yes	No
15.	Beth is engaged.	Yes	No
16.	Beth is married.	Yes	No

WORD STUDY.

Read the story.

Write the words with W.

w _ _ _

w _

w _ _ _

Write the words with G.

g _ _ _ _ _ _ _ _

g _ _ _

g _ _ _

Write the words with B.

B _ _ _

B _ _ _

Read the names. Put the names in the correct group.

Bill	Faye	Allen	Beth
Grace	Fred	Joe	Maria

Men's Names	Women's Names

AND YOU?

Read. Circle Yes or No.

1.	I am single.	Yes	No
2.	I am engaged.	Yes	No
3.	I am married.	Yes	No
4.	I am divorced.	Yes	No
5.	I live in the city.	Yes	No
6.	I work in the city.	Yes	No
7.	I live on a farm.	Yes	No
8.	I work on a farm.	Yes	No
9.	I am a farmer.	Yes	No
10.	I was a farmer.	Yes	No
11.	My father was a farmer.	Yes	No
12.	My grandfather was a farmer.	Yes	No

PERSONAL STORY.

Copy your Yes sentences.

_____

_____

_____

_____

_____

_____

_____

_____

ROSE SULLIVAN

My name is Rose Sullivan.
I have two daughters.
This is Ellen.
She is 7 years old.
This is Ruth.
She is 5.

I am divorced.
I do not have a husband.
It is a sad story.

Jim and I were married for 9 years.
We were not happy.
Sometimes Jim did not come home.
I was alone with my daughters.
I was unhappy.
I did not like my life.

CHECK YOUR UNDERSTANDING.

Read. Circle Yes or No.

1. Rose has two children.   Yes   No
2. Rose has a son.   Yes   No
3. Ellen is 9 years old.   Yes   No
4. Ruth is 7 years old.   Yes   No

5. Rose is divorced.   Yes   No
6. Rose has a husband.   Yes   No
7. Rose's story is happy.   Yes   No

8. Rose was married for 9 years.   Yes   No
9. Her husband's name was Tim.   Yes   No
10. Rose and Jim were happy.   Yes   No
11. Rose and Jim were unhappy.   Yes   No

WORD STUDY.

Write the opposites.

happy _ _ _

she _ _

wife _ _ _ _ _ _

son _ _ _ _ _ _ _

divorced _ _ _ _ _ _

unhappy _ _ _ _ _

Write the correct words. Copy the sentences.

1. Her _____ is Rose Sullivan.
     man   name

   _____

2. Rose has _____ daughters.
      two   tow

   _____

3. This _____ Ellen.
      is   it

   _____

4. It is a sad _____.
      store   story

   _____

5. Rose and Jim were _____ happy.
         no   not

   _____

6. Jim and Rose were married _____ 9 years.
                 for   from

   _____

AND YOU?

Read. Circle Yes or No.

1.	I am married.	Yes	No
2.	I am single.	Yes	No
3.	I am divorced.	Yes	No
4.	I have a husband.	Yes	No
5.	I have a wife.	Yes	No
6.	I have a child.	Yes	No
7.	I have children.	Yes	No
8.	I have a grandchild.	Yes	No
9.	I have grandchildren.	Yes	No
10.	I am happy.	Yes	No
11.	I am unhappy.	Yes	No

PERSONAL STORY.

Copy your Yes sentences.

_____

_____

_____

_____

_____

_____

_____

_____

TOM BAKER and LISA WASHINGTON

I am Dr. Tom Baker.

I am a doctor.

I am 42 years old.

I am married.

This is my wife.

Her name is Lisa Washington.

We do not have the same last name.

Lisa likes her family name.

I like my family name.

We have been married for 10 years.

We do not have any children.

Lisa is a manager.

She works in a department store.

We are busy and happy.

We like to do many things together.

CHECK YOUR UNDERSTANDING.

Read. Circle Yes or No.

1. Tom is a doctor. Yes No
2. Tom is single. Yes No

3. Lisa is Tom's wife. Yes No
4. Tom is Lisa's husband. Yes No
5. Lisa's last name is Baker. Yes No
6. Lisa's last name is Washington. Yes No
7. Lisa and Tom have been married for 1 year. Yes No

8. Lisa has a job. Yes No
9. Lisa is a manager in a department store. Yes No
10. Lisa is busy. Yes No
11. Lisa is happy. Yes No
12. Tom is busy. Yes No
13. Tom is happy. Yes No
14. Lisa and Tom have children. Yes No

WORD STUDY.

Read the words. Put the words in the correct group.

single	daughter	mother	married	father
wife	son	husband	divorced	grandfather

FAMILY	MARITAL STATUS
_____	_____
_____	_____
_____	_____
_____	_____

Write the correct words. Copy the sentences.

1. Lisa _____ a manager.
        is   this

   _____

2. Lisa and Tom do not have the same last _____.
                                 same   name

   _____

3. Lisa and Tom do not have _____ children.
         any   an

   _____

4. Lisa and Tom like to do _____ things.
         many   any

   _____

AND YOU?

Read. Circle Yes or No.

1. I am married.   Yes   No
2. I am single.   Yes   No
3. I have children.   Yes   No
4. I have grandchildren. Yes   No
5. I work.   Yes   No
6. I am retired.   Yes   No
7. I am busy.   Yes   No
8. I am happy.   Yes   No
9. I am unhappy.   Yes   No

PERSONAL STORY.

Copy your Yes sentences.

_____
_____
_____
_____
_____
_____
_____
_____

PERSONAL STORY.

Write your story.

My Family

_____
_____
_____
_____
_____
_____
_____
_____
_____
_____
_____
_____
_____
_____
_____
_____
_____

PERSONAL STORY.

HOME

Important words:

house	living room	furniture
apartment	dining room	bed
farm	kitchen	dresser
	bathroom	TV
	bedroom	stereo
	garage	radio

MARIA'S HOUSE

I live in a house.

My house has many windows.

My living room is very large.

I have many houseplants in my living room.

My favorite colors are blue and pink.

My curtains and carpet are blue.

My dining room has blue flowers
on the walls.

My kitchen is blue.

My bedroom walls are pink.
My curtains are blue.
My bed covers have blue flowers.
I think my house is beautiful.

CHECK YOUR UNDERSTANDING.

Read. Circle Right or Wrong.

1.	Maria lives in an apartment.	Right	Wrong
2.	Maria's house has many windows.	Right	Wrong
3.	Her living room is small.	Right	Wrong
4.	Maria has a big living room.	Right	Wrong
5.	Maria has many plants.	Right	Wrong
6.	The plants are in the house.	Right	Wrong
7.	Maria likes black.	Right	Wrong
8.	Maria likes pink.	Right	Wrong
9.	Maria likes blue.	Right	Wrong
10.	Maria's carpet is blue.	Right	Wrong
11.	Maria's kitchen is blue.	Right	Wrong
12.	Maria's dining room is white.	Right	Wrong
13.	The bedroom walls have pink flowers.	Right	Wrong
14.	The bed covers have pink flowers.	Right	Wrong
15.	Maria likes her apartment.	Right	Wrong

WORD STUDY.

Read the story.

Find the colors. Write them. Find the rooms. Write them.

Colors
_____
_____

Rooms
_____
_____
_____
_____

Write the correct words.

One	Many
room	_____
color	_____
kitchen	_____
wall	_____

Is or Are? Write the correct words. Copy the sentences.

1. Maria's living room _____ large.

   _____

2. Maria's favorite colors _____ blue and pink.

   _____

3. Maria's kitchen _____ blue.

   _____

4. Her bedroom walls _____ pink.

   _____

AND YOU?

Read. Circle Right or Wrong.

1.	I live in a house.	Right	Wrong
2.	I live in an apartment.	Right	Wrong
3.	My apartment is large.	Right	Wrong
4.	My apartment is small.	Right	Wrong
5.	My house is small.	Right	Wrong
6.	My house is large.	Right	Wrong
7.	I have a kitchen.	Right	Wrong
8.	I have a living room.	Right	Wrong
9.	I have a dining room.	Right	Wrong
10.	I have a bathroom.	Right	Wrong
11.	I have two bathrooms.	Right	Wrong
12.	I have one bedroom.	Right	Wrong
13.	I have two bedrooms.	Right	Wrong
14.	I have three bedrooms.	Right	Wrong
15.	I have many bedrooms.	Right	Wrong

PERSONAL STORY.

Copy the right sentences about you.

_____

_____

_____

_____

_____

_____

_____

GRACE and FRED'S HOUSE

Fred and I were married 42 years ago.
I was 25 years old and Fred was 23.
We lived with my parents.
Their house was very small.
Fred didn't like my mother.
My mother didn't like Fred.

We saved our money for 9 years.
We bought this house.
Our house is on a quiet street.
We have a front yard and a back yard.
We have three bedrooms, a kitchen,
a dining room, a living room, and
a bathroom.

Fred and I are old.
Fred doesn't cut the grass.
I don't like to clean the house.
I want to move.
I want a small apartment.

CHECK YOUR UNDERSTANDING.

Read. Circle Right or Wrong.

1.	Fred married Grace 24 years ago.	Right	Wrong
2.	Fred and Grace live with Grace's parents.	Right	Wrong
3.	Fred's house was very small.	Right	Wrong
4.	Fred liked Grace's mother.	Right	Wrong
5.	Grace's mother liked Fred.	Right	Wrong
6.	Fred and Grace saved their money.	Right	Wrong
7.	Fred and Grace bought an apartment.	Right	Wrong
8.	Fred and Grace bought a small house.	Right	Wrong
9.	Their house is on a busy street.	Right	Wrong
10.	They have a front yard.	Right	Wrong
11.	There is a back yard.	Right	Wrong
12.	Their house has two bedrooms.	Right	Wrong
13.	The house has five rooms.	Right	Wrong
14.	Fred cuts the grass.	Right	Wrong
15.	Grace likes to clean the house.	Right	Wrong
16.	Grace wants a big apartment.	Right	Wrong
17.	Grace wants to move.	Right	Wrong
18.	Grace likes the house.	Right	Wrong

WORD STUDY.

Read the story.

Find the rooms. Write them.

Rooms
_____
_____
_____
_____
_____

Write the opposites.

divorced _ _ _ _ _ _ _ 				back _ _ _ _ _

father _ _ _ _ _ _ 				large _ _ _ _ _

Combine the words. Copy them.

do not _ _ _ _ 			_____

does not _ _ _ _ _ _ 			_____

did not _ _ _ _ _ 			_____

Write the correct words.

1. Fred _____ like Grace's mother.

2. Grace's mother _____ like Fred.

3. Fred _____ cut the grass.

4. Grace _____ like to clean the house.

34

AND YOU?

Read. Circle Right or Wrong.

1.	I am married.	Right	Wrong
2.	I am single.	Right	Wrong
3.	I am divorced.	Right	Wrong
4.	I live alone.	Right	Wrong
5.	I live with my parents.	Right	Wrong
6.	My children live with me.	Right	Wrong
7.	I live with a roommate.	Right	Wrong
8.	I live with two roommates.	Right	Wrong
9.	I live in the city.	Right	Wrong
10.	I live on a quiet street.	Right	Wrong
11.	I live on a busy street.	Right	Wrong
12.	I live on a farm.	Right	Wrong
13.	I have a front yard.	Right	Wrong
14.	I have a back yard.	Right	Wrong

PERSONAL STORY.

Copy the right sentences about you.

_____

_____

_____

_____

_____

_____

_____

JOE'S APARTMENT

My apartment is on the second floor of this building.
I live with a roommate.
His name is Paul.
I don't see him very much.
He has a girlfriend.

I like my bedroom.
I have pictures on the walls.
I like baseball.
I keep my baseball things in a corner.
I sleep on a mattress on the floor.
It's comfortable.

The living room is very big.
We don't have a lot of furniture.
We bought some old furniture.
We have a TV, a stereo, and a radio.
Our apartment is really nice.

CHECK YOUR UNDERSTANDING.

Read. Circle Right or Wrong.

1.	Joe lives in an apartment.	Right	Wrong
2.	Joe lives in a building.	Right	Wrong
3.	Joe lives in a house.	Right	Wrong
4.	Joe's apartment is on the first floor.	Right	Wrong
5.	Joe's apartment is on the third floor.	Right	Wrong
6.	Joe has a roommate.	Right	Wrong
7.	His roommate's name is Paul.	Right	Wrong
8.	Paul has a girlfriend.	Right	Wrong
9.	His girlfriend's name is Paul.	Right	Wrong
10.	Joe has pictures on his bedroom walls.	Right	Wrong
11.	Joe likes baseball.	Right	Wrong
12.	Joe plays baseball.	Right	Wrong
13.	Joe's bed is comfortable.	Right	Wrong
14.	The living room is small.	Right	Wrong
15.	Joe and Paul have a lot of furniture.	Right	Wrong
16.	Their furniture is new.	Right	Wrong
17.	Joe and Paul have a TV.	Right	Wrong
18.	They have a stereo.	Right	Wrong
19.	They have a radio.	Right	Wrong

WORD STUDY.

Read the story.

Write the words with P.

P _ _ _

p _ _ _ _ _ _

Write the words with R.

r _ _ _ _ _ _ _

r _ _ _

r _ _ _ _

r _ _ _ _ _

Combine the words. Copy them.

do not _ _ _ _   _____

does not _ _ _ _ _ _   _____

it is _ _ _   _____

Write the correct words.

1. Joe _____ see his roommate very much.

   _____

2. _____ comfortable.

   _____

3. Joe and Paul _____ have a lot of furniture.

   _____

4. Joe _____ have new furniture.

   _____

38

AND YOU?

Read. Circle Right or Wrong.

1.	I live alone.	Right	Wrong
2.	I live with my family.	Right	Wrong
3.	I live with a roommate.	Right	Wrong
4.	My apartment is small.	Right	Wrong
5.	My apartment is big.	Right	Wrong
6.	My house is small.	Right	Wrong
7.	My house is big.	Right	Wrong
8.	I have a TV.	Right	Wrong
9.	I have a stereo.	Right	Wrong
10.	I have a radio.	Right	Wrong
11.	I have a lot of furniture.	Right	Wrong
12.	My furniture is old.	Right	Wrong
13.	My furniture is new.	Right	Wrong

PERSONAL STORY.

Copy the right sentences about you.

_____

_____

_____

_____

_____

_____

_____

ROSE'S MOBILE HOME

My daughters and I live in a mobile home.
It's small.

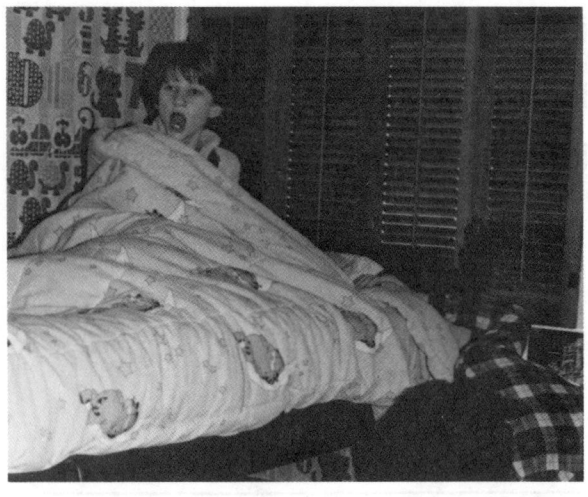

We have one bedroom.
My daughters sleep here.
They sleep in a bunkbed.
Ellen and Ruth don't have a dresser.
They keep their clothes in boxes.
I'll buy a dresser next year.

I sleep in the living room.
I have a sofa bed.
I open it at night.
The sofa becomes a bed.
I'm lonely.
I don't like to live alone with my daughters.

CHECK YOUR UNDERSTANDING.

Read. Circle Right or Wrong.

1.	Rose lives in a house.	Right	Wrong
2.	Rose and her daughters live in a mobile home.	Right	Wrong
3.	The mobile home is small.	Right	Wrong
4.	Rose has two daughters.	Right	Wrong
5.	There are three bedrooms.	Right	Wrong
6.	Rose's daughters sleep in the bedroom.	Right	Wrong
7.	Rose's daughters sleep in a bed.	Right	Wrong
8.	Ellen and Ruth have a dresser.	Right	Wrong
9.	Rose has a dresser.	Right	Wrong
10.	Rose bought a dresser.	Right	Wrong
11.	Rose will buy a dresser.	Right	Wrong
12.	Rose sleeps in the bedroom.	Right	Wrong
13.	Rose sleeps in a sofa bed.	Right	Wrong
14.	The sofa bed is in the bedroom.	Right	Wrong
15.	The sofa bed is in the living room.	Right	Wrong
16.	Rose opens the sofa bed at night.	Right	Wrong
17.	Rose is happy.	Right	Wrong
18.	Rose likes to live alone with her daughters.	Right	Wrong

WORD STUDY.

Write the sentences with different words.

1. <u>It</u> is small.
   _____

2. My daughters sleep <u>here</u>.
   _____

3. <u>They</u> keep their clothes in boxes.
   _____

Make the words singular.

One	Many
_____	daughters
_____	boxes
_____	beds
_____	bedrooms

Write the correct words.

1. Rose has two _____.
           daughter   daughters

2. Their clothes are in three _____.
           box   boxes

3. Rose has a sofa _____.
           bed   beds

4. The mobile home has one _____.
           bedroom   bedrooms

AND YOU?

Read. Circle Right or Wrong.

1.	I live in a mobile home.	Right	Wrong
2.	I live in a house.	Right	Wrong
3.	I live in an apartment.	Right	Wrong
4.	It is small.	Right	Wrong
5.	It is big.	Right	Wrong
6.	There is one room.	Right	Wrong
7.	There are two rooms.	Right	Wrong
8.	There are three rooms.	Right	Wrong
9.	There are four rooms.	Right	Wrong
10.	There are five rooms.	Right	Wrong
11.	There are six rooms.	Right	Wrong
12.	There are many rooms.	Right	Wrong
13.	I like my home.	Right	Wrong

PERSONAL STORY.

Copy the right sentences about you.

_____

_____

_____

_____

_____

_____

_____

LISA and TOM'S CONDO

Lisa and I work downtown.
We bought an apartment downtown.
Our building is very large.
There are 30 floors.
There's a swimming pool in the basement.
There's a garage, but we don't have a car.
We don't like to drive.

Our condo has 8 rooms.
Our living room is big.
We have an office.
Sometimes we work there.
There are two desks and many books.

Another room is a den.
We watch TV and listen to music there.
We also have a kitchen, a dining room,
two bedrooms, and a bathroom.
We like our condo.

CHECK YOUR UNDERSTANDING.

Read. Circle Right or Wrong.

1.	Lisa works downtown.	Right	Wrong
2.	Tom works downtown.	Right	Wrong
3.	Lisa and Tom live in the city.	Right	Wrong
4.	Lisa and Tom live in a small building.	Right	Wrong
5.	The building has a swimming pool.	Right	Wrong
6.	There is a basement.	Right	Wrong
7.	There is a garage.	Right	Wrong
8.	Lisa and Tom have a car.	Right	Wrong
9.	Tom likes to drive a car.	Right	Wrong
10.	Lisa likes to drive.	Right	Wrong
11.	Lisa and Tom have a condo.	Right	Wrong
12.	The condo is small.	Right	Wrong
13.	There are seven rooms in the condo.	Right	Wrong
14.	There is an office in the condo.	Right	Wrong
15.	They work in the office.	Right	Wrong
16.	Books are in the office.	Right	Wrong
17.	There are two desks in the den.	Right	Wrong
18.	They have a TV.	Right	Wrong
19.	There are two bedrooms.	Right	Wrong
20.	Lisa and Tom like their condo.	Right	Wrong

WORD STUDY.

Read the story.

Write the words with L.

| L _ _ _ |
| l _ _ _ _ |
| l _ _ _ |
| l _ _ _ _ _ |
| l _ _ _ _ _ |

Write the words with D.

| d _ _ _ _ _ _ _ |
| d _ _ _ _ |
| d _ _ _ _ |
| d _ _ _ |
| d _ _ |
| d _ _ _ _ _ |

Write the sentences.

1. we work downtown

   _____

2. we bought an apartment downtown

   _____

3. we dont have a car

   _____

4. we dont like to drive

   _____

5. our condo has 7 rooms

   _____

6. we like our condo

   _____

AND YOU?

Read. Circle Right or Wrong.

1.	I live in a condo.	Right	Wrong
2.	I live in a big house.	Right	Wrong
3.	I live in a small house.	Right	Wrong
4.	I live in a small apartment.	Right	Wrong
5.	I live in a big apartment.	Right	Wrong
6.	I live in a mobile home.	Right	Wrong
7.	There is a garage.	Right	Wrong
8.	I have a car.	Right	Wrong
9.	My car is small.	Right	Wrong
10.	My car is big.	Right	Wrong
11.	I can drive a car.	Right	Wrong
12.	I like to drive.	Right	Wrong
13.	I have a TV.	Right	Wrong
14.	I like to watch TV.	Right	Wrong
15.	I have a stereo.	Right	Wrong
16.	I like to listen to music.	Right	Wrong

PERSONAL STORY.

Copy the right sentences about you.

_____

_____

_____

_____

_____

_____

_____

THE MILLER'S FARM HOUSE

Our house is very old.
My grandfather built the house in 1890.
The house had two rooms.
There was a fireplace.
My grandmother cooked food in the fireplace.
The house didn't have a bathroom.
There was an outhouse.

My father made the house bigger in 1920.
My father built the second floor.
The bedrooms are on the second floor.
My father put electricity in the house.
My father put a bathroom inside.

I want to buy air conditioning this year.
Next year I want to buy new windows.
We like our house very much.

CHECK YOUR UNDERSTANDING.

Read. Circle Right or Wrong.

1.	Bill's house is very old.	Right	Wrong
2.	Bill built the house.	Right	Wrong
3.	Bill's father built the house.	Right	Wrong
4.	Bill's grandfather built the house in 1980.	Right	Wrong
5.	In 1890 the house had many rooms.	Right	Wrong
6.	The house had one room in 1890.	Right	Wrong
7.	Bill's grandmother had a stove.	Right	Wrong
8.	In 1890 the bathroom was outside.	Right	Wrong
9.	Bill's father built the second floor.	Right	Wrong
10.	Bill's father built the third floor.	Right	Wrong
11.	The bedrooms are on the second floor.	Right	Wrong
12.	The house had electricity in 1902.	Right	Wrong
13.	The house has electricity now.	Right	Wrong
14.	Bill wants new windows.	Right	Wrong
15.	Bill wants to buy a new stove.	Right	Wrong
16.	Bill wants to buy air conditioning.	Right	Wrong
17.	Bill wants a third floor.	Right	Wrong
18.	Bill wants another room.	Right	Wrong
19.	Bill likes the house.	Right	Wrong
20.	Bill's family likes the house.	Right	Wrong

WORD STUDY.

Make the words show the past.

Present	Past
build	_____
buy	_____
have	_____
make	_____
put	_____

Write the correct words.

1. Bill's grandfather _____ the house in 1890.
                   builds   built

2. The house _____ two rooms in 1890.
            has   had

3. Bill's father _____ the house bigger in 1920.
           made   makes

4. Bill's father _____ a second floor in 1920.
           built   builds

Read the words. Match the words. Write the new words.

fire	place	_____
grand	side	_____
grand	mother	_____
bed	father	_____
bath	room	_____
in	room	_____

AND YOU?

Read. Write the correct words.

1. I live in _____.

       a house   an apartment

       a condo   a mobile home

2. It is _____.

       very old   old

       very new   new

3. It is _____.

       very large   large
       very small   small

4. There are _____ rooms.

       two   three   four
       five   six   many

5. I _____ my home.

       like   do not like

Personal Story.

Copy the sentences.

_____

_____

_____

_____

_____

_____

PERSONAL STORY.

Write your story.

My Home

_____
_____
_____
_____
_____
_____
_____
_____
_____
_____
_____
_____
_____
_____
_____
_____
_____
_____
_____

WEEKDAY ACTIVITIES

Important words:

morning	wake up	go
afternoon	get up	come
evening	make	watch
night	eat	read
	drink	drive
breakfast	wash	sleep
lunch	take a shower	
dinner	work	
	talk	
gas station	teach	
factory	study	
school	meet	
restaurant	visit	
hospital		

JOE'S DAY

I wake up early everyday.
I live near a park.
I like to jog in the park.
I usually jog for 45 minutes everyday.
I even jog in the winter.
After I jog, I take a shower.

I work in a gas station.
I work the day shift.
I work from 8:00 to 4:00.

After work, I play baseball.
I always have a good time.
After the game I meet my friends.
We usually go to a restaurant.
We drink beer and eat pizza.
Sometimes we go to a disco.
We talk to the women.
I like to meet pretty women. I like to dance.

CHECK YOUR UNDERSTANDING.

Read. Circle True or False.

1. Joe's apartment is near a park.   True   False
2. Joe jogs in the morning.   True   False
3. Joe works in a bus station.   True   False
4. Joe plays baseball after work.   True   False
5. Joe likes to play baseball.   True   False
6. Joe eats dinner with his friends.   True   False
7. Joe eats dinner at home.   True   False
8. Joe likes pizza.   True   False
9. Joe likes to dance.   True   False
10. Joe likes sports.   True   False

Read the sentences. Write the sentences in the correct order.

A. Joe works.

B. Joe goes to work.

C. Joe wakes up.

D. Joe goes to a disco.

E. Joe jogs.

F. Joe meets his friends.

G. Joe eats pizza.

H. Joe takes a shower.

I. Joe plays baseball.

J. Joe dances.

1. _____
2. _____
3. _____
4. _____
5. _____
6. _____
7. _____
8. _____
9. _____
10. _____

WORD STUDY.

Read the story.

Write the words with J.

J __ __
j __ __

Write the words with SH.

sh __ __ __ __
sh __ __ __

Write the correct words. Copy the sentences.

1. Everyday Joe wakes _____ early.
        up   cup

   _____

2. Joe jogs for _____ minutes.
       45   54

   _____

3. Joe _____ a shower.
     makes wakes takes

   _____

Read the story. Write the sentences with different words.

1. <u>We</u> go to a restaurant.

   _____

2. <u>We</u> eat pizza.

   _____

3. Joe likes to dance with <u>them</u>.

   _____

56

AND YOU?

Read. Finish the sentences.

1. I wake up at _____.

2. I eat breakfast at _____.

3. I eat lunch at _____.

4. I eat dinner at _____.

5. I go to school at _____.

6. I leave school at _____.

7. I come home at _____.

8. I go to bed at _____.

Personal Story.

Copy the sentences in the correct order.

_____

_____

_____

_____

_____

_____

_____

_____

BETH MILLER'S DAY

I get up at 6:00.
Mom and I make breakfast.
After breakfast, Mom washes the dishes and I dry them.
Mom sweeps the floor and I make the beds.
Mom washes the clothes and I hang them up outside.

At 1:00 Dad drives me to work.
I work part-time in a store.
I'm a cashier.

My boyfriend picks me up at 6:00 and he drives me home.
Sometimes we eat dinner at my house.
Sometimes we eat dinner at his parents' house.
Sometimes we stay in town and see a movie.

CHECK YOUR UNDERSTANDING.

Read. Circle True or False.

1. Beth gets up late. True False
2. Beth and Mrs. Miller make breakfast. True False
3. Beth washes the dishes. True False
4. Mrs. Miller sweeps the floor. True False
5. Beth has a job. True False
6. Beth drives the car to work. True False
7. Beth works evenings. True False
8. Mr. Miller drives Beth home. True False
9. Beth leaves the store at 6:00. True False
10. Beth eats dinner with her boyfriend. True False

Read the sentences. Write the sentences in the correct order.

A. Beth goes to work.
B. Beth gets up.
C. Beth eats dinner.
D. Beth finishes work.
E. Beth makes breakfast.
F. Beth makes the beds.
G. Beth dries the dishes.
H. Beth eats breakfast.
I. Beth works in a store.

1. _____
2. _____
3. _____
4. _____
5. _____
6. _____
7. _____
8. _____
9. _____

WORD STUDY.

Read the story.

Write the words with TH.

th __ __
th __

Write the words with T.

t __
t __ __ __
t __ __ __ __

Write the words with S.

s __ __ __ __
s __ __ __ __
s __ __ __ __ __ __
s __ __ __

Write the opposites.

get up __ __ __ __ __

go __ __ __ __

girlfriend __ __ __ __ __ __ __ __ __

full-time __ __ __ __ - __ __ __ __

Combine the words. Write the new words.

some   times   _____

out   side   _____

in   friend   _____

boy   side   _____

part   time   _____

60

AND YOU?

Read. Circle True or False.

1.	I get up early.	True	False
2.	I get up late.	True	False
3.	I make breakfast.	True	False
4.	I eat breakfast.	True	False
5.	I wash the dishes.	True	False
6.	I dry the dishes.	True	False
7.	I make the bed.	True	False
8.	I go to work.	True	False
9.	I go to school.	True	False
10.	I study English.	True	False
11.	I go home.	True	False
12.	I make dinner.	True	False
13.	I eat dinner.	True	False
14.	I watch TV.	True	False
15.	I go to bed.	True	False

Personal Story.

Copy the true sentences about you. Write them in the correct order.

_____

_____

_____

_____

_____

_____

_____

MARIA'S DAY

I wake up at 5:30 every morning.
I feed my cat.
Then I take a shower, put on my make-up, and dress for work.

I'm a math teacher. I teach 7th grade.
I start work at 8:00 and finish at 3:00.
After work I go to an exercise class.
Then I go home.

I usually eat a salad for dinner.
I'm on a diet.
After dinner, I go to a French class.
I study French for two hours.
I get home at 9:00.
I check my students' homework.
Sometimes I watch TV.
I read in bed and fall asleep about 11:00.

CHECK YOUR UNDERSTANDING.

Read. Circle True or False.

1.	Maria wakes up late.	True	False
2.	Maria feeds her cat in the morning.	True	False
3.	Maria puts on her make-up after she showers.	True	False
4.	Maria teaches math.	True	False
5.	Maria teaches from 8:00 to 3:00.	True	False
6.	Maria exercises after work.	True	False
7.	Maria eats a big dinner.	True	False
8.	Maria is a French teacher.	True	False
9.	Maria has a TV.	True	False
10.	Maria reads at night.	True	False

Read the sentences. Write the sentences in the correct order.

A. Maria eats dinner.

B. Maria goes to her exercise class.

C. Maria takes a shower.

D. Maria gets up.

E. Maria teaches math.

F. Maria puts on her make-up.

G. Maria watches TV.

H. Maria feeds her cat.

I. Maria studies French.

1. _____
2. _____
3. _____
4. _____
5. _____
6. _____
7. _____
8. _____
9. _____

WORD STUDY.

Write the opposites.

fall asleep _ _ _ _ _ _

teach _ _ _ _ _

go _ _ _ _

start _ _ _ _ _ _

Write the correct words.

1. Maria _____ up at 5:30.
        wakes   makes

   _____

2. Maria _____ work at 8:00.
        stops   starts

   _____

3. Maria is a math _____.
        teacher   cheater

   _____

4. Maria likes to _____ salad.
        eat   tea

   _____

5. Maria _____ to a French class after dinner.
        goes   does

   _____

6. Sometimes Maria _____ TV.
        watches   washes

   _____

AND YOU?

Read. Circle True or False.

1.	I wake up early.	True	False
2.	I wake up late.	True	False
3.	I work the day shift.	True	False
4.	I work the night shift.	True	False
5.	I go to school.	True	False
6.	I stay home.	True	False
7.	I study English.	True	False
8.	I teach English.	True	False
9.	I study French.	True	False
10.	I exercise everyday.	True	False
11.	I jog.	True	False
12.	I watch TV.	True	False
13.	I clean my house everyday.	True	False
14.	I listen to the radio everyday.	True	False
15.	I do my homework everyday.	True	False

PERSONAL STORY.

Copy the true sentences about you.

_____

_____

_____

_____

_____

_____

_____

GRACE'S DAY

Fred and I wake up early every morning.
We can't sleep much.
I make breakfast.

Fred loves to fix old cars.
Every morning he goes to the junkyard.
He buys many old car parts in the junkyard.
He brings them home.
He works on his car all day.
Sometimes his friends come to visit.
They talk and fix the car.
They have a good time.

These are my neighbors Mary and Ann.
They are sisters. They live together.
Every afternoon I visit them.
We talk and watch TV.
On Wednesdays I go to an ESL program.
I'm a volunteer. I help the students.
The school doesn't pay me.
I like to help people.

CHECK YOUR UNDERSTANDING.

Read. Circle Right or Wrong.

1.	Grace sleeps late.	Right	Wrong
2.	Fred sleeps late.	Right	Wrong
3.	Fred likes cars.	Right	Wrong
4.	Fred fixes cars.	Right	Wrong
5.	Fred fixes cars in the junkyard.	Right	Wrong
6.	Fred brings home old car parts.	Right	Wrong
7.	Fred and his friends fix the car.	Right	Wrong
8.	Fred likes to talk.	Right	Wrong
9.	Grace visits her friends every morning.	Right	Wrong
10.	Mary and Ann are Grace's neighbors.	Right	Wrong
11.	Mary and Ann are sisters.	Right	Wrong
12.	Grace, Mary, and Ann like to talk.	Right	Wrong
13.	Grace watches TV with her neighbors.	Right	Wrong
14.	Grace goes to school everyday.	Right	Wrong
15.	Grace goes to an ESL program every Wednesday.	Right	Wrong
16.	Grace is a student.	Right	Wrong
17.	Grace studies English.	Right	Wrong
18.	Grace helps the students.	Right	Wrong
19.	The school pays Grace for her work.	Right	Wrong
20.	Grace likes to help people.	Right	Wrong
21.	Grace is happy.	Right	Wrong

WORD STUDY.

Read the story.

Write the words with V.

v _ _ _ _

v _ _ _ _ _ _ _ _

Write the words with CH.

_ _ ch

_ _ _ ch

Make the words plural.

One	Many
car	_____
part	_____
friend	_____
sister	_____
school	_____

Write the correct words.

1. Fred likes to fix old _____.
       car   cars

2. He buys many car _____.
       part   parts

3. His _____ come to visit.
       friend   friends

4. Grace and Mary are _____.
       sister   sisters

5. The _____ does not pay Grace.
       school   schools

AND YOU?

Read. Circle True or False.

1.	I fix old cars.	True	False
2.	I like to fix old cars.	True	False
3.	I work in my garage.	True	False
4.	I work in my house.	True	False
5.	I work in a school.	True	False
6.	I work in a factory.	True	False
7.	I work in a gas station.	True	False
8.	I work in a hospital.	True	False
9.	I work in a restaurant.	True	False
10.	I work outside.	True	False
11.	I visit my friends everyday.	True	False
12.	I like to talk to my friends.	True	False
13.	I talk to my neighbors everyday.	True	False
14.	I like to watch TV.	True	False
15.	I like to listen to the radio.	True	False

PERSONAL STORY.

Copy the true sentences about you.

_____

_____

_____

_____

_____

_____

_____

ROSE'S DAY

Everyday I wake up at 6:00.
I make sandwiches for my daughters' lunch.
They take their lunches to school.

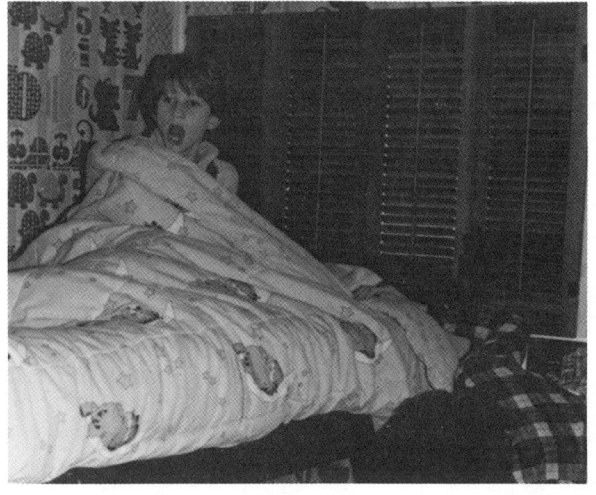

At 6:30 I wake up my daughters.
They make their breakfast.
They usually eat cereal and toast.
I make dinner in the morning because I'm not home at night.
I leave at 7:30.
I drive Ellen and Ruth to school.
Then I go to the factory.
At 4:30 I leave the factory.

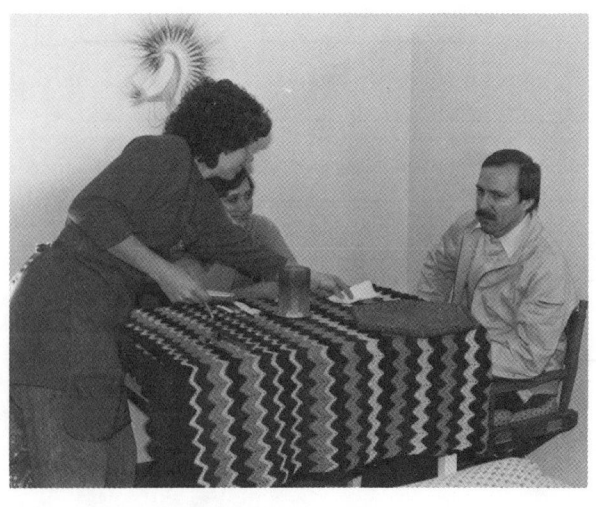

I drive to my second job.
I'm a waitress. I don't like the job.
My neighbor takes care of my daughters at night.
I come home at 11:00.
My daughters are sleeping.
My days are long.

CHECK YOUR UNDERSTANDING.

Read. Circle True or False.

1.	Rose wakes up early.	True	False
2.	Rose makes sandwiches for breakfast.	True	False
3.	Rose makes lunch in the morning.	True	False
4.	Rose takes her lunch to school.	True	False
5.	Ellen and Ruth get up at 6:30.	True	False
6.	Rose makes breakfast for her daughters.	True	False
7.	Ellen eats cereal and toast.	True	False
8.	Ruth eats dinner in the morning.	True	False
9.	Ellen makes dinner in the morning.	True	False
10.	Rose is at home at night.	True	False
11.	Rose leaves home at 7:30.	True	False
12.	Rose has a car.	True	False
13.	Ellen goes to school.	True	False
14.	Rose works in a factory.	True	False
15.	Rose works the day shift.	True	False
16.	Rose works in a restaurant at night.	True	False
17.	Rose has two jobs.	True	False
18.	Rose's daughters are alone at night.	True	False
19.	Rose works hard.	True	False
20.	Rose has a lot of money.	True	False

WORD STUDY.

Read the story.

Write the words with N.

n __ __

n __ __ __ __ __ __

n __ __ __ __

Write the words with C.

c __ __ __   c __ __ __ __ __

c __ __ __

Read the words. Write the words in the correct group.

breakfast   lunch   night
dinner   home   evening
factory   afternoon
morning   school

Meals	Places	Time

72

AND YOU?

Read. Circle True or False.

1.	I wake up early.	True	False
2.	I wake up late.	True	False
3.	I make breakfast.	True	False
4.	I eat breakfast.	True	False
5.	I work the day shift.	True	False
6.	I work at home.	True	False
7.	I make lunch.	True	False
8.	I eat lunch at home.	True	False
9.	I eat lunch at work.	True	False
10.	I eat lunch at school.	True	False
11.	I make dinner.	True	False
12.	I eat dinner at home.	True	False
13.	I eat dinner at work	True	False
14.	I eat dinner in a restaurant.	True	False
15.	I work the night shift.	True	False

PERSONAL STORY.

Copy the true sentences about you.

_____

_____

_____

_____

_____

_____

_____

LISA and TOM'S DAY

Tom wakes up at 6:00.
He makes breakfast for us.
I get up at 6:30.
After breakfast, Tom goes to the hospital.
I take a shower and dress for work.
I leave the house at 8:00.

Our housekeeper comes every morning at 10:00.
She cleans the house.
She washes and irons the clothes.
She buys food and cooks dinner.

I finish work at 6:30.
Tom and I meet at home.
We eat dinner together.
We talk about our work.
Sometimes Tom works evenings in the hospital.
Sometimes I work at home.
At 11:00 we usually have a drink and go to sleep.

CHECK YOUR UNDERSTANDING.

Read. Circle True or False.

1. Tom sleeps late.   True   False
2. Lisa makes breakfast.   True   False
3. Tom eats breakfast at work.   True   False
4. Lisa cleans the house.   True   False
5. Lisa and Tom have a housekeeper.   True   False
6. Tom cooks dinner.   True   False
7. Lisa works late.   True   False
8. Lisa and Tom work evenings.   True   False
9. Lisa and Tom like to talk.   True   False
10. Lisa and Tom like their jobs.   True   False
11. Lisa and Tom are happy.   True   False

Read. Copy the sentences in the correct order.

A. Lisa gets up.   1. _____
B. Tom goes to the hospital. 2. _____
C. Tom gets up.   3. _____
D. Tom makes breakfast.   4. _____
E. Lisa and Tom eat breakfast 5. _____
F. Lisa goes to work.   6. _____
G. Tom and Lisa eat dinner.   7. _____
H. Tom and Lisa come home.   8. _____

WORD STUDY.

Write the correct words.

1. Tom _____ up at 6:00.
       wake   wakes

2. I _____ breakfast.
       eat   eats

3. Tom _____ to the hospital every day.
       go   goes

4. The housekeeper _____ the house every day.
       clean   cleans

5. I _____ to school.
       go   goes

6. Tom and Lisa _____ dinner together.
       eat   eats

7. Tom _____ evenings.
       work   works

8. Tom and Lisa _____ about their work.
       talk   talks

Write the sentences.

1. sometimes tom works evenings in the hospital

   _____

2. sometimes lisa works at home

   _____

3. they talk about their work

   _____

AND YOU?

Read. Complete the sentences.

1. I get up at _____.
2. I eat breakfast at _____.
3. I eat lunch at _____.
4. I eat dinner at _____.
5. I go to sleep at _____.
6. I leave home for school at _____.
7. I finish school at _____.
8. I come home at _____.
9. I go to sleep at _____.
10. I study English from _____ to _____.

PERSONAL STORY.

Copy the sentences in the correct order.

_____

_____

_____

_____

_____

_____

_____

_____

PERSONAL STORY.

Write your story.

My Weekday Activities

_____
_____
_____
_____
_____
_____
_____
_____
_____
_____
_____
_____
_____
_____
_____
_____
_____